APOCRYPHA OF LIGHT

planet earth poetry

This book is part of the Planet Earth Poetry
library at Hillside Coffee and Tea.

Poetry is meant to be shared.
Enjoy this book for a week or two.

Bring it back to Hillside Coffee and Tea
1633 Hillside Avenue in Victoria, BC

Please write your name and contact
information on the sign out sheet.

planetearthpoetry.com

BOOKS BY LORNA CROZIER

POETRY

Inside Is the Sky (1976)

Crow's Black Joy (1979)

Humans and Other Beasts (1980)

No Longer Two People (with Patrick Lane) (1981)

The Weather (1983)

The Garden Going On Without Us (1985)

Angels of Flesh, Angels of Silence (1988)

Inventing the Hawk (1992)

Everything Arrives at the Light (1995)

A Saving Grace (1996)

What the Living Won't Let Go (1999)

Apocrypha of Light (2002)

ANTHOLOGIES

Desire in Seven Voices (2000)

Addicted: Notes from the Belly of the Beast
(with Patrick Lane) (2001)

APOCRYPHA OF LIGHT

LORNA CROZIER

M&S

National Library of Canada Cataloguing in Publication Data

Crozier, Lorna
Apocrypha of light

Poems.
ISBN 0-7710-2483-5

I. Title.

PS8555.R72A86 2002   C811'.54   C2001-903938-7
PR9199.3.C76A86 2002

We acknowledge the financial support of the Government of
Canada through the Book Publishing Industry Development
Program for our publishing activities. We further acknowledge
the support of the Canada Council for the Arts and the Ontario
Arts Council for our publishing program.

Typeset in Garamond by M&S, Toronto
Printed and bound in Canada

McClelland & Stewart Ltd.
The Canadian Publishers
481 University Avenue
Toronto, Ontario
M5G 2E9
www.mcclelland.com

1 2 3 4 5   06 05 04 03 02

For my mother, who believes,
and for Patrick, who inspires

APOCRYPHA OF LIGHT

CONTENTS

Mind was out there – the first thing God had made, but it refused to shake itself from darkness, to sing or howl or bow before him. So God made Pen and said, *Describe mind with your strokes and cursives. Tell me what it is.* Pen lay still as if it were nothing more than what it appeared to be – a plucked white feather, a fleck of blood at its tip. *Draw mind,* God said. *If you can't describe it, show me what it is.* Pen preened, then gazed into the distance and didn't move. *All right. Draw anything you like,* God said, *but think of mind while you do it, the huge intelligence that will dream me into words.* Pen began to fill the page with specks so small and black and close together it looked as if the feet of flies had been dipped in ink. That was the beginning of dust, the beginning of the earth. Pen spilled a drop that dribbled and swerved from side to side. That was the beginning of rivers.

It sketched plants, birds, beasts, and every living thing, and God was pleased. Then it drew a man and woman made from sticks. *Stop,* said God. *We have to agree on mind. These, you understand, will be its keepers; it will dwell inside them. You must draw mind before you place them in the world.*

Pen sighed and looked at God. It drew an arrow from the dots that were the earth and wrote *MIND!* It drew an arrow from the squiggle that was river and wrote *MIND!* It drew arrows from the lilies of the field, from crow, from water snake, from brome, from stone, from tortoise and wrote *MIND, MIND, MIND!* pressing so hard it broke through God's thick parchment –

where there was nothing but space,
where there was nothing but darkness,
colossal and silent, it wrote *MIND!*

God finally understood. He breathed over all that Pen had made and hoped he wouldn't regret it. There was something disturbing about Pen. Something annoying about its certainties, its exclamations. If it could take God's first creation, a thing as marvellous as mind, and scatter it in all directions, what would it do next? God considered snapping it in two and sealing it inside a mountain with a guard of lesser seraphim. Better yet, he'd return it whence it came, bury it among the blazing quills of Lucifer, his most beautiful, most brilliant angel. The safest place, God thought, for Pen to be.

BOOK OF ORIGINS

Is there any *thing whereof it may be said, See, this* is *new?*
it hath been already of old time, which was before us.

– Ecclesiastes 1:10

APOCRYPHA OF LIGHT

On the first day, light said
Let there be God.
            And there was God.
Light needed shape to move inside,
a likeness tawny and thick-maned.
It strode into the absence we call night
and what it tongued
sparked visible then glowed,
warmed by its golden spittle.

It splashed and rolled in water
till rivers and seas could not be parted
from its gleam. It lingered:
        on the hourglass
        of August pears; on blackbird,
        bear scat, calves' blood;
        on the hand of the beloved,
        its unlikely flare.

It went everywhere, glossed all
that waited to be seen. At last
it slipped into the farthest corner –
there, it stumbled. Stopped.
Hid its brightness and would not move.

What in the dark did it wish it hadn't found?

Not arbutus limbs, an otter's head
just above the sea; not orange pips,
fish fin, a panther's muscled plush.

Now you make a list of things.
Remember light's likeness, remember
this is the beginning of the first day.

THE ORIGIN OF THE SPECIES

> . . . but the old man only said that it was pointless to speak of there
> being no horses in the world for God would not permit such a thing.
>   – Cormac McCarthy, *All the Pretty Horses*

Drenched with dawn
eohippus, smaller than a fox,
walked out of chaos.

She struck the sand. Water
gushed from her hoofprint,
drops flying through the air

and where they fell
the sky came down to rest
and a thousand miracles of grass

meadowed the desert.
For centuries eohippus lived
satisfied and self-contained

then her legs and muzzle lengthened,
muscles pushed against
her withers, thickened her neck.

Now, ready for the wind
she made it lean and boneless,
its mane and tail visible

across the sky. Imagine
horse and wind
in the sun's warm pastures

before the fall. Imagine
the two of them alone
adrift in the absolute

beatitude of grass,
no insect biting,
no rope or bridle.

In the mornings of that lost
and long ago beginning,
nothing broken

or in need of breaking.

LESSON IN PERSPECTIVE

The cat creates world
with a paw's touch, with a stroke of whiskers,
intricate parallels like a lesson in perspective
where no lines meet.

The colours are those a cat can see,
the many greys and sepias of shade,
the sun's glossolalia on blades of grass
quivering in the slightest breeze.

After warbler and nuthatch,
after thrush, chickadee, and finch,
the cat makes mouse, bumblebee, and spider,
then the dragonfly that beats
on the rilled roof of his mouth,
a word with wings.

The cat makes words with fangs, too,
with hooves, fins, and tusks.
At dusk he says a word that moves
so lightly across the mind
it must be a small, nectar-sipping moth,
feet of such delicate design
it walks on petals and leaves no bruise.

THE START OF THE BLUES

Leaving the garden, the snake
drags its old skin behind it
like a long smoky breath
trapped inside a saxophone,
the first saxophone
in the world.

GOD'S YES AND NO

From the silence above
the undivided water,
with his larynx, mouth, and glottis
God shaped *Yes* and *No*.

Pleased with what he'd said,
he tucked them in an empty scroll
long enough to unroll itself
around the earth.

From all their loud begettings
God expected little yes's, little no's
to march from end to end –
a line of red ants and of black –
but when he cast his eyes across
the watermarked papyrus
there were words he'd never seen before.

It seemed a small annoyance.

He didn't know
this would be the end of the straight answer.
The end of yes to his commandments.
The end of no to Satan.

Before he spat in clay
and pinched into shape
Those-Who-Would-Obey-Him,
they had a language waiting –

maybe, kind of, guess so,
yeah but, almost, I don't know . . .

SNOW

If snow had its way
there'd be only cold
and two colours: dawn's slow
improbable blue and the animals
all white – polar bear, winter hare,
and holy ghost
with its old unblinking eyes,

the wide brush of its wings
visible in fields though
that word would not exist,
nothing ever planted. So, too,
with *leaf, violet, goldfinch,*
snow's singular season
crystalline, unchanged.

If it allowed room for you
what creature would you be?
Your breath the first thing
you see each morning,
the last at night.

Easy to lose yourself
in snow's way of thinking –
going from nowhere to nowhere
light-footed
on the smallest, coldest stars.

INVENTIONS OF THE LESSER GODS

Warts,
earwax, hic-
cups, the little
toe, wisdom
tooth.

A PROPHET IN HIS OWN COUNTRY

The gopher on his hind legs
is taut with holiness and fright.
Miniature and beardless,
he could be stoned or flooded out,
burnt alive in stubble fields,
martyr to children for a penny a tail.

How can you not believe an animal
who goes down headfirst
into darkness, into the ceaseless
pull of gravity beneath him?
What faith that takes!

I come to him with questions
because I love his ears, how perfectly
they fit, how flat they lie against his head.
They hear the inner and the outer
worlds: what rain says
underground. The stone's praise
for the sparrow's ankle bone.

Little earth-otter, little dusty Lazarus,
he vanishes, he rises. He won't tell us
what he's seen.

EVOLUTION IN MOONLIGHT

Always you come back to the moon:
old man, bull's horn, winter hare,
the thin body of an ancient god
placed there on the tongue.

What will you say then?
Stars are wasps dipped in silver.
They chew holes in the darkness
to build their paper nests.

What will you say then, that taste
dry and holy in your mouth?

Here it is moonlight.
You walk the garden paths,
your hands shiny as scales
as if you are only
on your way to being human,
still smelling of the sea.

What you've called a soul
hovers just beneath your skin.
Or has it left your body?
And now walks
beside you, bright-eyed
and feline, each paw placed

so carefully
on the rain-slicked grass, the way
a new god enters the world.

Why is her name not spoken?
Why is a lock of her hair, a knuckle bone
not placed on our hearth, our altar?
We hear her breath in wind we walk into,
backwards and blind. We hear our dried
and brittle cauls she rattles through the night.

Into the world she pulls us – an ox
dragging the blades of a wooden plow.
Out of the world she pulls us – a lion
tugging sinews from around
the stubborn heart.

We live on the milk of God's
mother, and do not know it.
Milk of meadows, milk of rivers,
thin milk of winter moons.

When Moses called out, *Who is like thee,*
glorious in holiness, fearful in praises,
doing wonders? the Lord of his fathers
did not say her name.

BOOK OF TALES

Those Bible stories and words weren't the kind you forgot. It was like they'd happened to you all along, that they were your own memories. You didn't always know what they meant, but you did know how they felt.

– Tim Winton, *Cloudstreet*

WHAT THE SNAKE BRINGS TO THE WORLD

Without the snake
there'd be no letter *S*.
No forked tongue and toil,
no pain and sin. No wonder
the snake's without shoulders.
What could bear such a weight!

The snake's responsible for everything
that slides and hisses, that moves
without feet or legs. The wind, for example.
The sea in its long sweeps to shore and out again.

The snake has done some good, then.
Even sin to the ordinary man
brings its pleasures. And without
the letter *S* traced belly-wise
outside the gates of Eden
we'd have to live
with the singular of everything:
sparrow, ear, heartbeat,
mercy, truth.

ORIGINAL SIN

1. The First Woman

We were mothers giving birth
to each other, or we were sisters,
our home the night's vast womb.
We orbited inside its silky
black cocoon. If Galileo had been
there with his telescope
and blasphemy, he would have named
our double brightness
and I wouldn't have been so lost.

My hand reached out
and to prove I was the first
the angels tied it with a strong red string,
the origin of scarlet as a curse.
I felt her grow beside me, her spirit curve
against my bones like cream inside a spoon.

We were one creature then,
four-legged, perhaps a fawn
whose hooves had not grown hard,
a calf so strange we would be kept
inside a jar. Then I counted fingers,
counted toes, and she looked back at me.

I, not Eve, brought pain into the birthing room.
I didn't want to leave her. I clung to the womb
with my nails and teeth, ripped night from day,
eternity from now.

That was my first argument with God.
The second: I wouldn't lie placid
as a hooked and fatty fish under Adam,
my wings pinned back. For punishment
God banished me and turned my sister into bone,
honed away everything she'd been
when we lay together among stars.

Some nights I wait at the edge of the garden –
how lush it is, how full of anguish.
Light and docile, she walks toward me,
a trail of creatures at her side.
Does she know I'm here? She's forgotten

my face, forgotten our one smell
as we wound around each other,
her fingers in my mouth, my hand
holding her heartbeat, a wounded wren
I cannot save from grief.

2. The Fall of Eve

When the animals used to talk to me –
lisp of snail, click of grasshopper's
exact consonant – there were rumours
a woman with wings roamed the wasteland.
They said she was furred, sleek and shimmering
as a weasel, eyes wells of desert water
where you'd surely drown.

Not knowing what she feared, I washed
the smell of man from my skin,
walked to where the garden stopped
and everything Adam couldn't name
fell into poetry and silence.

Beside the hawthorn hedge, the forbidden
tart on my tongue, I said *Lilith*
though I didn't remember
what it meant, then I said *Beloved*
and something like a breath lifted
the hair on the back of my neck.

Before I could turn, God's voice
roared through the leaves
and I glimpsed her wings unfolding,
feathers bewildering the sky.
My own arms rose and I know
the way you know your own sorrow

on this earth, once I was that dear,
that close to her,
once I too could fly.

And the waters prevailed upon the earth an hundred and fifty days.
 – Genesis 7:24

Every living thing
a nightmare, me and my two brothers
rounding them up, dumb creatures fighting
the net and crate. Torn and bitten,
we had no time to heal. I thought
my skin would never close.

Food enough for forty days and nights
but when the heavens shut, the ark still drifted
through an endless blue – a maddened mind –
five more months on water. Even if we'd known,
there'd have been no room,
every hold and cranny crammed with life.
My wife so sick, her hair came off in swatches.

I started with the Dodo and the Auk, males first.
Their mates had one more chance to lay,
then they went, too. Passenger Pigeon,
Sage Hen, Dusky Seaside Sparrow.
Easiest to take the gentlest – Blue-Faced
Lemur, Mountain Hare, the Unicorn
who bowed when we came near.
The final weeks were harder:

Sabre Tooth, Three-Toed Sloth, Prairie
Grizzly, Manticore, its violent human grin.

My brothers, Ham and Japheth, sawed off
the heads. We planned to show our children's
children what had been before.
Though we hid them from the sun, they blackened.
The stench more than we could bear,
one night we threw the heads into the sea.

They floated like living creatures
who'd surfaced to watch us pass, eyes
stunned with moonlight. Our faces, too,
all that could be seen above our robes
that kept one kind of cold away.

WOMAN WITH BEARS

(for Tiff)

Noah's wife stepped inside the hold's
pungent dark. Sleep-walking,
when she woke she was stroking
the wide forehead of a bear.
He was weeping, his muzzle wet, his mate
a denser darkness behind him in the cage.
What to do but keep on stroking till the animal
lowered his head to her lap and closed his eyes.
She slept as well and when she woke,
a bear snored on either side. One could be death,
the other tenderness. She thought of the son
killed at her breast for his wet fur head.
One could be pity, the other desire. She thought
of her husband, smooth and hard in their bed;
one could be terror, the other grace.
Could she rise without disturbing such a sleep?
Wade into the world as it had been: bears in the woods
pawing berries, she on the porch with the cat in her lap,
the baby curled in her womb's watery cage.
One could be forgiveness; the other, love.
Nothing resembles what this one knows.

TOWER OF BABEL

And the whole earth is of one language
and one speech. Deer talks to woman
and woman to fox, no mistrust or fear.
Magpie chats with muskrat, and oh,
the grass! How wet and eloquent
its green jive with the rain.
If a man hates, he says so. If a child
needs love she mouths the word
and it moves warmth around her.
Even the husband understands his wife's
impatience, the names she cries in sleep,
and she, in turn, hears his childhood
on the tip of his tongue, holds him
for the lost ordinary boy he was.
Sometimes his voice draws water
from that place, fresh and clear.
How close he comes to God then,
how close to grace.
One language and one speech.
What a time this is on the plains of Shinar!
What a sound in heaven's ears!
Surely *Babel* will forever mean
the radiance and candour of the word.

THE BARRENNESS OF SARAH

> Behold now, I know that thou art a fair woman to look upon: . . .
> when the Egyptians shall see thee, that they shall say, This is his
> wife: and they will kill me. . . . Say, I pray thee, thou art my sister:
> that it may be well with me for thy sake.
>
> – Sarah's husband, Abraham, Genesis 12: 11-13

Old women sold to Pharaoh when they were young
bathed me in water heated by the sun, soothed
my breasts and thighs with petals bruised for beauty –
lotus, asphodel, white gardenia. How gentle these
women with my skin, how brown their fingers.

Smaller than my husband and sad-eyed, Pharaoh lay
so light upon me I seemed to rise, what stayed below,
my shadow moving. Above his cries I heard the howl
of plagues let loose like heaven's hounds.
His people dying one by one, he called to Abraham,
What hast thou done? Why didst thou call her sister?

My body riven, Abraham rode me south to Bethel,
he rich with Pharaoh's gold for our one god, the fattest
cattle, she-asses, and camels about to birth.
In my womb I felt a quickening, Egypt craving life.
Each day I took a poison as the women of my tribe
for centuries have done. Within a week
what finned and flickered no longer moved.
I had to drag myself from death, rinse the venom

from my mouth. Many who did this did not survive –
my aunt, my younger sister, my mother's friend.
Skin tinged yellow they were buried at the river's bend.

Abraham denied me one more time.
It was written Abimelech, King of Gerar,
did not touch me. Three nights
he drew aside the curtains of my bed.
We left his land with sheep and oxen,
my husband's pouches heavy with
a thousand silver pieces, pitiless price.
I knew I'd die from poison. Instead I bit
on leather, pounded my belly with a stone
until the blood swam out.

I was ninety when the Lord told Abraham
I would conceive. Scolded for my laugh
I laughed again when the angels visited my tent,
Isaac's seed a spark that flashed from them
to me. My womb burned new as any girl's
before she knows a man, before she holds
those little deaths deep inside her flesh.

LOT'S DAUGHTERS

From Sodom's gates our father
brought two strangers home.
He bade our mother bake them bread,
my sister wash their feet and me
to dry them. I held our softest cloths,
those saved for my first bleeding.

No wings or brilliant scales or eyes
so fierce they burned your skin
as our father's often did.
I thought him wrong to call them angels
until I buffed their feet to brightness.
Long and pale they looked so new –
as if they'd never walked or felt a stone
beneath them. My hands still hold their shine.

Before our father broke the bread,
from up and down the street, neighbours
who'd seen the strangers at the gate
stormed the house, shook their fists
and shouted, *Send them out!*
Father said he'd not release them
but he had two daughters still at home
to do with as they pleased. Both of us
too young to marry, my breasts small
as apricots set out to dry,

a few hairs only on the soft rise
between my sister's legs.

I confess I prayed he'd send her out
and I'd be saved, fists pounding
the walls, our mother wailing,
clutching us so tight I thought
she'd pull us through her skin.
It was then the strangers raised
their hands and smote the wicked
blind, not our father and not me
for wishing what I did about my sister,
but the men outside who wanted them.

I wish we'd all been blinded. Then,
our mother wouldn't have turned
to see her other daughters one last time,
the two who wouldn't leave because
their husbands mocked our father's warning.

I taste my mother in everything I eat
and in my tears, and in the blood
I touched my fingers to
when our father, drunk on wine,
took my sister then came to me,
outside Sodom and Gomorrah.

THE SACRIFICE OF ABRAHAM

Imagine the boy a goat,
pupils horizontal,
his laugh a bleating
wind shepherds through the grass.

I still count those seconds
when I raised the knife:

sunlight blinking
on his belly. God's terrible
desire to see the heart fly out.

Everything after
                    comes from this.

THE SACRIFICE OF ISAAC

I bind my breasts with hide. Eat a jackal's heart
and ride in dust to the mountains of Moriah.
Three nights I sit with what they cannot see
beyond their fires. Though I'm close enough
to touch his cheek, I will my hands to stillness.
Before dawn, our last day on the road, a caravan
stutters by, heavy with its load like something
from the past. I am too old for them to trouble me
though a boy rides up, tips his goatskin
and offers me a drink. He drops his eyes
when I unveil my mouth, the darkness there.
I swallow his breath with water from his father's well,
mumble a blessing though I do not know
his gods, their indifference or their lust.
When the groan of wheels fades, I hear
my child's laugh ringing through the grass
like bells tied to the morning wind.
He is climbing. Bent double under wood,
he bears his fire upon his back.
I wait by a thicket, tufts of ram's wool
on the brambles, knife cold against my thigh,
until the altar's built, Isaac asking,
Father, where's the lamb?
then I step into the open, fists on fire,
above my swinging arm
the bare throat of my husband's
Lord opening in a flood of crimson light.

THE WILD BOY

Though there is nothing
you can see,
you feel the heat of his gaze
from the shadows of the redwood,
the mirrors of trembling aspen;
and the old brain in you
knows a quickening in the marsh
where everything is half-submerged
and his heavy head
lifts its rack and courses the air.

Believe, if you will,
nothing lived before the garden.
Believe, if you will, a man
is different from a bear, a woman
from a kestrel; believe the crow
flattened on the freeway is not
the son of god.

Call him Cain, call him Esau,
Ishmael, Enkidu. He is the one
who sniffs your hair, lays
his furred hand upon your forehead
as you dream. He tucks his black hoof
in the arch of your foot and lifts your leg.
Are you still sleeping?
You are right to be afraid.

His mouth is full of wolf's milk,
his mind is dark water
running under ice. Believe
if you will, Adam and Linnaeus.
This is the only way he knows
to get back home.

DINAH, JACOB'S DAUGHTER

The afternoon four of my brothers
tied me to a tree, bound my skirts
over my head like a sack so I couldn't see,
I thought nothing worse could happen.

Years later in Canaan
the prince's son raped me.
He's made you a whore,
my brothers said,
and then they killed him
and every man in the city.
Don't think it had anything
to do with love.

There were ten of them,
older than me.

Every night it seemed
when we were kids,
our parents sleeping,
one of them would
hold me down,
another mount me,
doing nothing really
but pressing his hard
dense body on top of mine.
Baa like a sheep,

one of them whispered,
and we'll let you go.

Baa, I said, *baa*,
a third brother's hand
over my mouth.

Other things have been thrown down:
the head of a donkey, a broken wheel
caked with clay, the black hair of a woman
whose scalp was shorn the morning after
her wedding night. Hours of darkness
slide down without a sound. Tonight
he feels lucky to be deep in the ground
and still alive, lifting his face to the rain.

At dawn something lands at Joseph's feet.
It takes some time for him to touch it – a baby
cold and blue, thin cord dangling. Why
didn't he dream this, he wonders, instead
of sheaves and the lights of heaven bowing?

If he hears the pulley's creak and turn,
he'll make himself so wanted he'll be water
lifted to another's mouth, he'll be the earth's
salt rising. He wills himself to dream
he's in the bottom of a stone throat
that will spit him out if he finds the words
it needs to say: the donkey whole again,
rolling in dust on the village road,
the baby rocking in arms that want to hold it,
and in his tent a woman on her knees above him,
swathing his face in her long black hair.

WHAT I GAVE YOU, TRULY

I am speaking from the other side
of the bramble bush, the side where nothing
grows but wheels and cogs and the loneliness
of exile on this earth. I am speaking
in the voice of thorns, the voice of wire,
though once I was a softness longed for
at the end of day, its vesper song,
mothering the weary. What I gave man
without a lie and truly, what I give you now
is Gravenstein, Spartan, Golden Delicious.
Eat this, I say, and your eyes open
as mine did then, all things innocent, unused,
my new man naked before me.
Remember that.
I give you the apple and you see
your lover for the first time, this wonder
repeated in the flesh. *Eat this*, chew
more sweetness before the bitter seeds,
the hard star at the core. I am speaking
in the voice of crow, the voice of rain. Stark naked
I am out here in the large and lovely dark,
the taste of you, the taste of apple in my mouth.

BOOK OF GOD

For I am the first and the last.
I am the honored one and the scorned one . . .
I am the silence that is incomprehensible . . .
I am the utterance of my name.

– "Thunder, Perfect Mind,"
The Nag Hammadi Library in English

GOD THE FATHER

Goes to the Legion every night
though he's not a veteran of the Wars,
leastways not the ones these old men
gab about. No Joshua or Moses here,
just Jackie Rosslin with his wooden leg,
his Victoria Cross, and those wraiths
who shiver once a year around the cenotaph.
God's the little man who sits alone,
nursing his beer, sometimes a shot of rye
at his elbow, a pack of Export A's tucked
in one shirt pocket and in the other, three
ballpoint pens in case there's something
to write down. Though his hearing's not
the best, he's the guy with the good eye,
unbeatable at shuffleboard and pool.
Truly, he could see a sparrow fall
if he'd a mind to, spot a single hair
on the toe of a shrew. It's a hard job
flirting with the barmaid every night
in a harmless way while the weekend toughs
challenge him at pool, bodies so tense
you'd think their lives depended on it.
They slap their quarters on the wood,
match him beer for beer until they can't
stand steady. He never shows them mercy
even when they've lost so much by midnight
they're meek enough

to inherit some small corner of the earth.
There's always one, though, who bitches
the old man wins because he owns the tables,
knows the cues. God the Father keeps his peace
though sometimes he'd like to throw
a lightning bolt across the room, flood the town
and start it over. . . . Maybe not. They don't know
they've got it good. No one's died here of retribution,
a violent act, unless you count Mack Goldman's
heart attack (when he fell he never broke
his glass of rum), or the blood vessel
that exploded in Bob Sawatski's brain
the second his dart hit the bull's eye.
No one's soul's riding on the eight ball
or swept up like the quarters God collects
then rolls in thin brown strips
when the barmaid calls last round.
Even so, there's one thing
you'd better believe in – God's good eye –
an aim so bee-lined he can reach from heaven
and tap Adam's finger
just to prove he's got the touch.

GOD THE MOTHER

Cleans the fancy house
on top of the hill Wednesday mornings.
The job's not bad, she tells her daughter,
who often feels ashamed. It helps to see
what those who prosper make of love
and earthly beauty. Though they lack
for nothing (as she's heard the woman say)
the couple's fighting all the time, the kids
think they're hard done by. She dusts,
then she vacuums, but mostly she picks up
what they've abandoned, even things
they're capable of seeing and cannot
live without. You'd hardly know she's there;
but just her glance stays the gardener
in his tasks. The seedlings flare, and a scent
like winter jasmine washes over him.
Upstairs, God the Mother strokes the coat
dropped in a heap and barely stops herself
from breathing life into the pelts, hundreds
of mink unstitching, rivering silver over oak
and Oriental rugs in their humped, hungry way.
Last week when the husband rubbed against her
as she cleaned the sink, she turned and
showed him for a second who she was.
The sun broke like bricks
through all the windows. He knocked against
the scrub pail and his hands flew open,

letting go of something he didn't know
he'd been clutching all his life. Now
though everything has changed, he remembers
only the dampness of his shoes, the dirty water
rim around the cuffs of his trousers,
and the woman who does day work
mopping up the spill.

GOD THE SON

Rushes to the rink
after school and early mornings,
canvas bag slung across his shoulders.
He's the Chosen One, the coaches say,
a Natural. His body on its blades skims weightlessly
across the blue lines. Later there'll be more
but for now the Grade 10 girls adore him.
They clip his picture from the paper, tape it
under cling-wrap above their beds, the large scar
visible, face ripped from teeth to cheekbone.
Not one of them could tell you what *icing* means,
let alone, *Sanguina Christi.*
Last season, right knee cracked, he hobbled
behind the bench, his adolescent body
suspended between crutches, palms stinging
from holding on that tight. One of the girls
brought him a Coke, another would've licked
the sweat from his upper lip if she'd been dared.
Forsaken, he thought it was forever – this thirst
for ice, his thighs' pull and thrust toward the goal,
the bang into the boards like the boom of thunder
when the sky ignites. Now, lacing up his skates again,
giving everything he is at every practice
as they dicker over what he's worth,
he prays before that kiss betrays him
he'll make the NHL.

A year or two maybe she'll design a cure,
a new theory of cosmogenesis,
but for now she just wants to be thirteen.
She wants the start of summer, early sixties,
small-town Saskatchewan. She'll admit
she even likes her brother though she wishes
she were older, not the other way around.
Most days you can't tell her from her friends –
a block from home she lights up, three times over
rolls the waistband of her skirt or the cuffs
of her new jeans even when it's minus twenty
and like any girl her age, she practises the words
she cannot say at home. Tonight after watching Elvis
in Hawaii at the Eagle Theatre where two years ago
she laughed at Ma and Pa Kettle on the farm,
a boy will touch her breasts in the back seat
of his father's car. Part of her will float away,
detached, ironic, but the rest begins to feel
a fierce, mute longing
that's as close to human as she'll ever get.
It guides her hand to touch him there,
her breath falling from so high above
for the first time she knows
clearly what she is inside this body,
this sad song drifting from the radio,
the angels who remember
bending down to hear.

FALLEN ANGELS I

A pause in conversation
and you hear them:
an owl's soft explosion
when it strikes what moves
across the snow, that sudden
punch when tinder's set on fire.
The weeping comes after.

It is the kind of weeping a woman does
after making love to a man
she has grown old with,
that moment when she senses most
the certainty of loss, the body
with its flawed grace falling
through the seven spheres
of loneliness
back into the known world.

They're the ones who shufflewalk,
feet close to the ground,
stirring up dust, or on linoleum
the heels of their slippers slapping
like idiot tongues, tendons slack.

These are the lame ones
with crutches or a heavy shoe,
arms plastered in casts
autographed with names like Gabriel,
Raphael, Michael, Abaddon.

They're afraid of stairwells
in tall apartment blocks, swayback
roofs and haylofts, the sinking sun.
Without exception they've never won
a game of Snakes and Ladders.

No matter where they've landed
they fall –
            off the wagon, on hard times,
out of favour, in love too easily.

Often, they turn to arson,
set fires in garbage bins and sheds,
in houses where a family may be sleeping.
Not that they hate the place they've come to

or loathe their human neighbours. Not that they love
the multifoliate flames budding from their fingers.

They do it because of the smoke,
they do it because smoke rises.

His face could be a skull
carved featureless from crystal,
or a death mask not allowed to set,
nose, cheekbones, forehead
blurred in the clay's slow slip.

Perhaps it's the face
of that Old World cousin
no one can identify – the boy
who stepped away from the rest
into the sun the second
the camera clicked.

Or maybe it's your father
who chose this blankness
so he won't startle you
with what he has become.
So many years without a razor, a cigarette,
so many years of speaking
without a mouth.

Think again of that boy in the photograph
dancing from one light to another,
the face no one remembers,
a fiery smudge.

WHO IS SHE, THEN?

She knew each beast and all the secret names
of tree and star and every bird in flight.
All things to her were different and the same.

She scrolled from alphabets of wind and rain
the wasps of winter and a blossom's blight.
She knew each beast and all the secret names,

the ice that glows inside the smallest flame
when snow in darkness spins the whole world white.
All things to her were different and the same.

She wrote in air the magpie's thin refrain,
its breviary made of bones and spite. She knew
each beast and all the secret names.

Who is she then who knows each creature's pain
and how it makes an opening for light?
All things to her are different and the same:

This dust is mother of the orphaned rain,
a full moon wears the barn owl's face in flight.
She knows each beast and every secret name.
All things to her are different and the same.

1. God's Mouth

That prairie sky you rhapsodize
is one huge yawn. He's bored
with what you're doing here.

Like a tone-deaf kid
who's been told
he carries a tune in a sieve,
God mouths the words.

The animals of course
can hear him. Look at that dog
who stares into the night,
his ears on fire –

it's God's great singing.

2. His Feet

It's his son's we're familiar with,
long and pale, pegged together.
God prefers the black
foot of the magpie, each toe
distinct and deftly clawed.
Other times he wants
a millipede's multiplicity.

When he walks as human,
under his robes his big toe's
fat as any sea lion,
his little one, blunt and pink
as that famous pig
crying all the way home.

What a journey! Gone so long,
no matter how many boots,
how many feet
he wears out and makes new,
he can't remember the bend
in the road by his mother's house
or the river where she bathed him.
He can't remember she used to
kiss each toe.

3. His Eyes

Alone in the bush
you feel something
     watching
from above or behind

a gaze so intense
                    it knuckles
up your spine
and burns
the base of your skull.

When you turn
                    you see

because cougar
deer or bear sees you

myopic, two-legged,
          radiantly grace-
less in God's eyes.

4. His Hands

So much ravelling
and unravelling,
the scrubbing of souls,
the peeling and plucking.

So much doing
and undoing,
the baking of bread
and the tearing apart
when the winged-ones gather.

5. God's Ear

Can we agree it's big?
If he pressed it to the ground
to listen for the armies coming,
a whole country
with its towers and fields
could live inside it.

So what's the reason
he doesn't hear us?

His ears are made of granite?
Plugged with wax?

Or is he waiting for
the one true word
that will come,
if it comes,
with early darkness?

The teeth in the mouth
of the speaker
grass-stained and worn.
The gold hairs around the lips
wet with water
when the head lifts

into such a listening

6. Untitled

He claims in fact it's
the socket of an eye,
a second anus,
a prim pursed mouth
that talks to creatures
living neither up nor down
but in the middle kingdom.

He'd never say
it was a navel.

You can see why.

7. God's Heart

It's tempting to say
he doesn't have one.

Otherwise,
what of the soft throats
of the lambs, the white
bulls – their startled blood?

That's to say nothing
of the other things
written inside
your book of grief.

Maybe his heart is thin,
maybe his heart is
made of hunger.

It comes into the world
as fox or goshawk,
or that winter tree
stripped clean of pity

branches bare of anything
that warms or blossoms
or makes them
break.

8. God's Bones

His bones are light,
they are light walking,
light sitting
and standing still.

If he dies
you can't bury them.
Light slips out of
any darkness. In pine
it becomes the pine;
in oak it gathers in the grain.

If he dies
you cannot cremate them.
They are fleshed with fire,
fire-fattened.

Even the smallest bone
in his inner ear –
there's enough light
for the whole world
to read by.

BOOK OF PRAISE

To praise the sun is to praise your own eyes.
Praise, the ocean. What we say, a little ship.

– Rumi, *The Essential Rumi*

The plains are a mind thinking slowly.

It's you the plains recall,
the way you strode across the earth

when you lived that open, sky
splitting around your shoulders and doubling

back: bicameral, long-winded. Day-dreamer,
you wouldn't have noticed if your feet

were blistered or baptised by the rain.
Nothing here defeats you. Again, it's all

in the walking, small figure on a road
going West. This is how the great plains see you.

All that slow thinking that surrounds me
thinking of you.

Remember the heart. Little mole.

My heart's as blind but sometimes
it's a winter hare. Soft-pawed and quick

it follows you in daylight and can't be
seen. You suspicious of sentiment,

its poverty and pride. Instead
you gave me a stone worn by water

so a chain slipped through.
It sat in the hollow of my throat

until I lost it. Remember the hare
invisible in snow, the little mole?

Star-nosed and dusty, he knows
at least two doorways to the light.

Blow wind. The bell is lonely.

The bells I've heard in summer
sound different when they ring

across the cold. I invite the magpie
from the spruce to break bread,

his cry not what you would call
a song, he's so much

made of winter. Beguile me
wind, even if you're bitter.

The bells are waiting:
their hoods of hoarfrost.

Now we are anyone. This coming to love.

This grey brings no sustenance.
Only the dead attend to their gardens

under the snow. The sky's so low
it drapes across the fields –

an old woman's loosened hair.
That's what the wind untangles

and combs across the highways.
Weather takes a nasty turn –

wind chill, white-out, no
rum or candles in my survival kit

and I'm four storms
from seeing you.

Give yourself the light.

Night comes quickly
but the snow gives off so much shine

it's not as dark as where you are,
the big trees leaning in.

Who will explain the bones?

Under the ice the creek yawns
and flexes its muscles, one by one.

Precipitous, the crows are back.
They pack away their sombreros

in the attic of the spruce, gossip
and natter at the magpie who

gives nothing away. Feathers
and bones he stayed all winter

in his black and white.
When he lifts from the branch

he sees his shadow moving –
another kind of brightness.

There is no road without you.

Believe me, everything's lost.
I wake – the road's not there.

Or the tractor . . . or the haystacks.
The countryside's been seeded

by an albino farmer
and his team of tundra swans –

four a.m., an airy whistling,
I thought it was the wind.

Have you seen the road?
That's the million-dollar question.

Here's another:
dressed in white, impatient

as a waitress in a small-town diner,
morning asks, *What's your pleasure?*

If I have to think about it
I shouldn't be here.

Teach me the stars. The way to summer.

Snow brings down constellations
without number.

No one names them.
What relief! Sinking in starlight,

I walk to the creek,
mouth stoppered with ice.

They call the water Wolverine
though I haven't seen the animal

or his tracks. Just the deer's,
silk-screened. Small moves

towards spring: their hoofprints,
the shape of maple seeds.

This is what is meant by noise. Tell me! Tell me!

The chickadee cries,
Tell me, me, me

through the windbreak.
Sweet nuisance, it follows

though I have no seeds or secrets.
Is this how you feel

when I need you so? My body
a begging bowl and blind.

Everything vanishes –
I try to hold a piece of ice.

Tell me. The early-morning snow's
a drawn-out sigh,

the sky rolled in cotton batting.
Is there a cure beneath it?

Valetudinarian, I almost faint
when the chickadee

sits on my palm,
its small exquisite weight

voluptuous. The black claws
on each foot thinner

than the finest nib. They make
the same sound, scratching.

How the mind works, works, works.

Intricate scrolls along the fencelines,
illuminant, elegiac. The curious

scripts of mice and rabbits:
their coming and their going.

Teresa of Avila said, *Learn to pray
not with noise but with longing.*

Prayers, then, in the pawprints.
I learn to read them

with my fingers,
in poor light and in good.

Welcome wise one. Tell me a story.

Today the snow is indecisive,
says both *yes* and *no* to falling

yet it chalks just one side
of the elms – magnetic north.

You could throw away
your compass, get lost in me.

I live between two places
like these elms, their proper name

Siberian. Babushkas,
hidden icons white with flour. Poems

learned by heart and eaten with the gruel.
Mandelstam! You'd be so welcome.

In this catholic garden no one lights
the caraganas' candelabra. Native

to Siberia too, they're no strangers
to hard labour. All day long, thin-

barked and twisted,
they break the stony wind.

Excellence in the small. Tears frozen on your face.

Winter: *eat the little, talk a lot —*
that's magpie's definition.

Tears freeze on the cheeks and
never fall. This is cold, not sadness.

Somewhere warmer, Vallejo said
we must learn

a different way of weeping. For now,
the old way will have to do.

My mouth between your legs. O flesh!

I admit it – I licked your hand-
writing, words made flesh, my tongue

stained black as if I'd sucked
a licorice stick. Now your letter's

impossible to read. Like the magpie.
Like the heart. You can have

that scavenger. Noisy magus,
he grants me nothing

with a sweep of his tail.
I'm sick of this undoing,

greenless miles of snow,
the coyote's scat red with rosehips.

Right now I'd trade the open
and all my braggadocio about the cold

for the little dogs
in raincoats on Dallas Road.

As the line moves. The leap! Thrashing there.

Night's flurry and fall.
The warp and woof of silence

upon waking, each thread
thick with frost and ecstasy.

At last! The sun glints
in every crystal. Shattered

starshine, mica, glass –
light throwing punches

oracular and quick
from every corner. It bruises

the eye, beauty
too small a word for what's

so radiant and fast.
The heart

can't hide in
such a light. It casts

its shadow with the rest,
flat-out and blue.

The geese in the south raise their heads in praise.

Have they begun their journey
to the nesting grounds? If I could

I would warn them, too soon,
too soon. Is there nothing you can do?

Everything's still hard here
under the moon. Wind makes it swing

on hinges like a sign made out of tin.
Truly, I can hear it creaking.

The body also moves
before the beloved has prepared

the fires and feasting.
When I raise my head it is you

I praise, this waking into wind's
slow change of seasons,

wings lifting under the great
glittering belly of the Bear.

ACKNOWLEDGEMENTS

Some of the poems have appeared in the following magazines: *Grain, Descant, Event, The Southern Review, Queen's Feminist Review, Poetry Wales, Thylazine, Prairie Fire, Atlantis, The Canadian Forum, Nimrod, Fiddlehead,* and *Carousel,* and in the anthology *Breaking the Surface.* The poems in the final section, "Book of Praise," were commissioned by CBC Radio's "Between the Covers" and aired on that program in the fall of 2000.

"Woman with Bears" was inspired by a scene from Timothy Findley's *Not Wanted on the Voyage.* The titles for the individual poems in "Book of Praise" are lines from Patrick Lane's book of poetry *A Linen Crow, A Caftan Magpie.* My poems in this section are a response and a tribute to this brilliant and unique collection.

I'd like to further acknowledge Patrick Lane for his belief in me, his love, and his poet's eye. Jan Zwicky, the remarkable editor of this collection, was a joy to work with. This book owes much to Ellen Seligman and the unerring copy-editing skills of Heather Sangster. Thanks to my friends in poetry, especially Elizabeth Philips, Eve Joseph, and Jane Munro; the Saskatchewan Writers'/Artists' Colony; and the University of Victoria's Centre for Studies in Religion and Society, which awarded me a fellowship to begin this manuscript. Thanks also to the University of Victoria for the travel grants that allowed me to attend the colonies at St. Peter's Abbey in Saskatchewan. And finally, thanks to my mother, who made sure I went to Sunday school, where my love of the Old Testament began.

82